Aa

acorn
An acorn is the seed from which an oak tree grows.

aeroplane
An aeroplane is a machine that flies. It has wings and engines.

aisle
An aisle is a space we can walk along between rows of seats or desks.

alligator
An alligator is a large crawling animal with four short legs and a long tail.

anchor
An anchor is a heavy piece of metal with a rope. It holds a boat in one place.

angel
An angel brings messages from God and is very good.

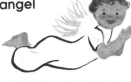

animal
An animal is any living thing that can move. A plant is not an animal.

antelope
An antelope is a kind of deer. It has long horns and can run very fast.

ape
An ape is a large monkey that lives in trees. Apes have no tails.

apple
An apple is a round fruit that grows on a tree. It is good to eat.

apron
An apron is a piece of material that we wear to keep our clothes clean.

ark
Noah saved his family and the animals from the flood in an ark.

arm
An arm is one of the two upper limbs of our bodies that we use for lifting things.

arrow
An arrow is a long stick with a point. We shoot arrows from a bow.

artist
An artist is a person who paints pictures.

athlete
An athlete is a person who takes part in sports. This athlete is jumping a hurdle.

awning
An awning is a canvas cover that keeps out the sun or rain

axe
An axe is a tool that people use to chop up wood.

B

baby
A baby is a very young child. Babies cannot walk or talk.

bag

A bag is a sack made of paper, cloth or plastic.

baker
A baker is a person who makes bread, biscuits and cakes. He bakes them.

ball

A ball is a round object. We play golf, football, tennis and cricket with a ball.

balloon
A balloon is a bag filled with air so that it will float.

banana

A banana is a long fruit with a thick yellow skin. We peel off the skin to eat the part inside.

bank
A bank is a thing we keep money in. This a bank in the shape of a pig. It is a piggy bank.

barber

A barber is a person who cuts and washes people's hair.

barn
A barn is a large building on a farm where grain and hay are stored.

barrel
A barrel is round and has flat ends. We keep things in barrels.

basket

A basket is made of wood or straw or wire. We can carry things in baskets.

bathtub
When we wash ourselves all over, we take a bath. We take a bath in a bathtub.

bead

A bead is round and has a hole through it for string. We wear beads round our necks.

bean
A bean is the long green part of a special plant. It is a vegetable that is good to eat.

bear

A bear is a large wild animal with a furry coat, flat paws and a short tail. Bears are black, brown or white.

bed
A bed is a piece of furniture with a soft part on which we sleep.

bee

A bee is an insect that flies. It has four wings. Some bees make honey.

beetroot
Beetroot is the root of the red beet plant. It is a vegetable that we eat.

B

bell

A bell is like a metal cup. When we shake a bell, it makes a ringing sound.

bib

A bib is a napkin that baby wears round his neck when he eats.

bicycle

A bicycle is a machine that we ride on. It has two wheels and pedals that we push.

bird

A bird is an animal with feathers and wings. Most birds can fly. A robin is a bird and so is an ostrich.

blackboard

A blackboard is a smooth piece of board that we write or draw on with chalk.

block

A block is a toy. Baby plays with blocks. These blocks have numbers and letters on them.

boat

When we travel on water we travel in a boat. A boat floats and moves on top.

book

You are reading a book. A book is made of paper and has a cover. We read stories in books.

boots

We wear boots to keep our feet and ankles dry and clean. Boots are made of leather or rubber.

bottle

We keep liquids like milk in a bottle. Bottles are made of glass or plastic.

bowl

A bowl is a deep round dish. We keep sugar in a bowl, and we eat some kinds of food from a bowl.

boy

A boy is a male child. A boy grows up to be a man.

broom

A broom is a brush with a long handle. We use a broom to sweep the floor.

brush

A brush is a tool with bristles. We smooth our hair with a hair brush. We paint with a paint brush. We clean our teeth with a tooth brush.

bubbles

Bubbles are little balls of air in a liquid. We make soap bubbles by blowing soapy water through a ring.

bucket

A bucket is like a pail. We keep water or coal in a bucket. It has a handle so that we can carry it.

bun

A bun is a round piece of baked bread that we eat with jam or with a hamburger.

bus

A bus is a large machine that takes people from one place to another.

butcher

We buy meat from a butcher. A butcher cuts up dead animals.

butter

Butter is a food that is made from milk. We eat butter on bread.

cabbage

A cabbage is a vegetable with large leaves. A cabbage is red or green.

cabin
A cabin is a small house made of wood.

cage

We keep birds in a cage to stop them flying away. A cage is made of metal.

calf
When a cow is young it is called a calf.

camel

A camel is a large animal that carries people across the desert. It has a large hump on its back.

camera
When we take a picture on holiday, we use a camera. It is a machine for taking pictures.

camp
A camp is a group of tents. Boys and girls go to Guide camp and Scout camp.

butterfly
A butterfly is an insect that flies. Butterflies have four lovely coloured wings.

button

A button is a piece of metal or plastic that we use to fasten our clothes.

canary
A canary is a small yellow bird that sings sweetly. When a canary is a pet it is kept in a cage.

candle

A candle is a stick of wax with a string running through it. The string burns and gives light.

cane

A cane is a stick that some people use to help them walk.

canoe
A canoe is a boat with pointed ends. It is pushed through the water with a paddle.

cap

A cap is a small hat with a peak at the front that shades the eyes.

car
A car is a machine that takes a family from one place to another.

card
A card is made of stiff paper and has a picture. We get cards on our birthdays.

C C

carpenter
A carpenter is a person who makes things with wood.

cheese
Cheese is made from the thick part of milk and is good to eat.

carrot
A carrot is a long thin vegetable with an orange root that grows underground and that we eat.

cherry
A cherry is a small, round fruit. Cherries are red, black or yellow.

cart
A cart is a vehicle with two wheels that we use for carrying things.

chest
A chest is a large box with a lid. We keep things in a chest.

castle
A castle is a large building with high walls and towers to keep the people inside safe from attack.

chicken
A chicken is a large bird. We eat the meat of chickens. A female chicken is a hen.

cat
A cat is a small furry animal that is kept as a pet. It belongs to the same family as lions and tigers.

chimney
A chimney is a wide pipe that takes smoke up into the sky.

caterpillar
A caterpillar is a butterfly before it is fully grown.

chimpanzee
A chimpanzee is a large brown ape. It has large teeth and paws that look like hands.

celery
Celery is a vegetable that you can eat either raw or cooked.

church
A church is a building where we go to worship God on Sundays.

chair
A chair is something we sit on. Sometimes a chair has arms.

circle
A circle is a ring that is perfectly round.

chalk
Chalk is a kind of soft stone that makes a mark when we write on a blackboard.

circus
A circus is a big show with animals who do tricks and clowns who make us laugh.

C

clock

A clock shows us what time it is. It is a machine that measures time.

closed

When something is closed it is not open. A lid closes a jar so that it is not open to the air.

clothes

We wear clothes to cover our bodies to keep us warm. Gloves, jackets and jeans are clothes.

cloud

A cloud is lots of tiny water drops in the sky. Clouds are white or grey.

clown

A clown wears bright clothes and paint on his face. He makes us laugh at the circus.

coach

A coach is a very comfortable bus. People go on long journeys in a coach.

coal

We burn coal to give us heat and power. Coal is found under the ground.

coat

A coat is a garment with sleeves. We wear coats over other clothes. This is a blue coat.

coffee pot

Coffee is a drink made from the seeds of a tree that grows in warm places. Coffee is made in a coffee pot.

collar

A collar is the bit of a dress or coat that goes round your neck. This collar is white.

colour

Yellow is the colour of a banana. Blue is the colour of the sky, and green is the colour of grass.

colt

A colt is a young male horse. A colt has long legs.

comb

A comb is a long piece of metal or plastic with teeth. We use a comb to smooth our hair.

cone

A cone is a shape that is round at one end and pointed at the other. This is a cone for ice cream.

cook

We make food ready to eat by heating it. We cook it. A person who cooks food is a cook.

corn

Corn is a yellow grain that grows on a tall plant. Corn is good to eat.

cornet

A cornet is made of metal. When you blow into a cornet it makes a musical sound.

cot

A cot is a bed with high sides. A baby sleeps in a cot so that he won't fall out.

C

cow

A cow is a large animal that lives on a farm. We get milk from a cow.

cowboy

A cowboy is a man who looks after cows in the West of the United States of America.

cradle

A cradle is a cot with bits of shaped wood on the bottom so that it rocks from side to side.

crayon

A crayon is like a pencil. It is made of wax or chalk. We colour pictures with crayons.

daisy

A daisy is a flower. It has white petals that grow around a yellow centre.

dandelion

A dandelion is a wild plant that has a bright yellow flower.

deer

A deer is a gentle, graceful wild animal that can run fast. A full-grown male deer is called a stag. He has horns.

dinner

Dinner is when we eat most food every day. We eat dinner in the evening or in the middle of the day.

dish

A dish is something we use to hold food. Cups and plates are dishes.

crown

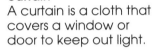

A crown is a band of metal and jewels worn by a king or queen.

cup

A cup is a dish for holding a drink. This is a cup for tea or coffee.

curtain

A curtain is a cloth that covers a window or door to keep out light.

cut

When we use scissors with paper we make it into pieces. We cut it.

D

dog

A dog is an animal that we keep as a pet or for work. Some dogs are small and others are large.

doll

A doll is a toy that looks like a little girl or boy.

donkey

A donkey is an animal that looks like a horse with long ears. We use donkeys to carry loads.

door

A door is the entrance to a house, or a room, or a cupboard.

doughnut

A doughnut is a round, sweet, fried cake with a hole in its centre.

dress
A dress is what girls wear as clothes. A dress has a skirt.

drum
A drum is a musical instrument. It is hollow inside, and we play it by beating it with sticks.

duck
A duck is a bird with webbed feet. Ducks live near water. The meat of a duck is good to eat.

eagle
An eagle is a large bird that eats other birds and small animals.

elephant
An elephant is a very large wild animal. It has two ivory tusks and a long trunk to pick up food and water.

elf
An elf is not a real person. He is a kind of fairy who appears in stories.

engine
An engine is a machine that makes things work. A car has an engine to make it move.

fairy
A fairy is an imaginary person, like an elf. Fairies appear in fairy stories.

family
A family means a father, a mother, and their children. Sometimes a family means all our relatives.

dunce
A dunce is a person who is not good at learning.

dustpan
We use a dustpan to gather the dust that we sweep off the floor with a broom.

dwarf
A dwarf is a person who is much smaller than other people.

envelope
An envelope is a cover made of paper which we put letters into.

equal
Equal means the same or just alike. The pieces of this pie are equal in size.

Eskimo
An Eskimo is a person who lives in the far north of America where it is always very cold.

eye
An eye is what we see with. We see with our two eyes.

farm
A farm is an area of land where food is grown and animals are kept.

farmer
A farmer is a person who owns a farm or who works on it.

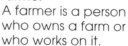

feather

A feather is one of the bits of the covering of a bird. A feather is very light.

fence

A fence is made of wood, metal, or wire. We use fences to keep animals in or out.

fern

A fern is a plant that has pretty leaves but no flowers.

fire

A fire burns things. It gives heat and light.

fish

A fish is an animal that lives in water. Most fish are good to eat.

flag

A flag is a cloth with a pattern that has a special meaning. This is the flag of the United States of America.

flamingo

A flamingo is a large bird with long legs and a long neck. It has lovely pink feathers and lives near water.

game

The children are playing a game. They are playing by rules.

garage

A garage is a building where we keep a car.

flowerpot

We grow plants and flowers indoors in a flowerpot. It is a pot for growing things.

flower

A flower is the part of a plant that blossoms and makes seeds. Flowers have many colours and shapes.

fly

A fly is a common insect with two wings. We usually see flies only in warm weather.

fork

We use a fork to pick up food. It has a long handle and prongs for holding the food.

fox

A fox is a wild animal that looks like a dog. It has a red furry coat.

frog

A frog is a small wild animal that lives on land and in water.

fruit

A fruit is the part of some plants that holds seeds. Many fruits are good to eat.

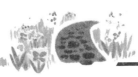

garden

A garden is a piece of ground where flowers and vegetables grow.

gate

A gate is a part in a fence that opens to let us through. It is like a door.

gift

We give people gifts. Everyone likes to get a gift for their birthday.

giraffe

A giraffe is a wild animal with a very long neck. Giraffes eat leaves from tall trees.

girl

A girl is a female child. A girl grows up to be a woman.

glass

Glass is a hard material that we can see through. It is easy to break. This is a drinking glass.

glasses

Glasses help us to see things. Glasses are made of a special kind of glass. They are also called spectacles.

glove

A glove keeps a hand warm. There are two gloves, one for each hand.

goat

A goat is an animal with horns and a little beard. Goat's milk is good todrink.

hammer

A hammer is a tool. We use a hammer to hit nails into things.

hand

A hand is at the end of an arm. We have two hands. which we use to do lots of things.

goldfish

A goldfish is a small, orange or gold-coloured fish. We usually keep goldfish in a tank.

goose

A goose is a large bird that can swim. A goose lays eggs. The meat of geese is good to eat.

grapefruit

A grapefruit is a large yellow fruit. Grapefruit is good to eat for breakfast.

grape

A grape is a fruit that grows in bunches. Some grapes are purple and some green.

grass

Grass is a plant. It has long, narrow green leaves and grows on the ground.

grocer

A grocer is a person who sells food. A grocer works in a shop that is called a grocery.

gun

A gun is a machine that shoots balls of metal. A gun is a weapon that kills.

handkerchief

A handkerchief is a piece of cloth or paper that we use to wipe our nose and eyes.

hat

This is a man's hat. He wears his hat on his head to keep it warm.

hatchet

A hatchet is a small axe. It has a short handle. We use a hatchet to cut wood.

hay

Hay is grass that has been cut and dried. In winter, farmers give animals hay to eat.

hen

A hen is a female bird. Hens lay eggs, which are good to eat. The meat from a hen is called chicken.

hobbyhorse

A hobbyhorse is a toy horse made of wood.

hoe

We use a hoe to dig up weeds and to loosen earth in the ground. A hoe is a garden tool.

ice

Ice is frozen water. It is hard and cold. We make ice to keep things cold.

ice cream

Ice cream is made of cream, milk, eggs, and sugar. We freeze it to make it cold.

ice skates

Ice skates are boots with blades on the bottoms so that we can move on ice.

igloo

An igloo is a little house made with blocks of ice. Eskimos live in igloos.

holly

Holly is a bush that grows shiny green prickly leaves and red berries. We decorate with holly at Christmas.

honey

Honey is a thick sweet liquid. Honey is made by bees.

hook

A hook is curved so that it holds or catches things. We hang clothes on the brown hook. We use the black hook to catch fish.

horn

A horn is an instrument that makes a noise when we blow into it.

horse

A horse is a large animal used for working or for riding. A cowboy rides a horse.

ink

Ink is a coloured liquid in a pen. We write and draw with ink.

insect

An insect is a tiny animal. Some insects crawl. Others have wings and can fly.

iron

An iron is a machine that we heat and use to take the creases out of our clothes.

island

An island is a piece of land with water all round it. Britain is an island.

Jack-in-the-box
A Jack-in-the-box is a toy that jumps out of a box when we open it.

jaguar
A jaguar Is a large, fierce wild cat with a spotted coat.

jam
Jam is a sweet food. It is made from fruit, sugar, and water. We spread jam on bread.

kangaroo
A kangaroo is a large wild animal that lives in Australia. It has strong back legs for jumping.

kettle

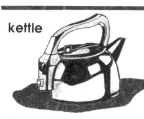

We use a kettle to make water hot. It is a pot with a lid, a handle and a spout to pour water through.

key
A key is a piece of metal that fits into a keyhole. We use a key to lock or unlock a door.

kid

A kid is a young goat. The skin of a kid is made into a soft leather.

lace
Lace is a fine material made of threads that we use to make clothes look pretty.

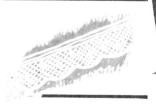

ladder

A ladder is what we use to climb up things. It is made of two long pieces of wood or metal joined by rungs.

jar

A jar is made of glass. We keep food in a jar with a lid. These peaches are in a jar.

jug
A jug is what we keep liquids in. Milk and water are kept in jugs.

juice

When we squeeze an orange we get juice. Juice is the liquid part of oranges and other fruits.

king

Some countries have a king. The king is the man who rules these countries. He wears a crown.

kite
A kite is a toy that flies in the wind. It has a long tail and a long piece of string that we hold on to.

kitten

A kitten is a young cat. Kittens like to play with wool.

knife
A knife has a metal blade that is sharp. We use a knife to cut things.

lamb
A lamb is a young sheep. The meat of a lamb is good to eat.

lamp

We burn oil or heat a wire in a lamp to make light so that we can see at night.

L

l

lantern
A lantern is a lamp with glass sides and a handle. We use a lantern outdoors at night.

leaf

A leaf is one of the green flat parts that grow on plants.

lemon
A lemon is a fruit. It is sour, not sweet. We make lemonade from lemon juice, sugar and water.

letter

A letter is a message that we write to someone. We put a letter in an envelope and post it.

lettuce

A lettuce is a vegetable with large green leaves. We eat lettuce in a salad. We do not need to cook it.

lighthouse
A lighthouse is a tall building beside the sea. It has a light to warn ships of rocks.

magazine

A magazine is a kind of book with a paper cover. This is a children's magazine.

man
A man is a grown-up male person. Daddy is a man. A boy grows up to be a man.

marbles

Marbles are round balls made of coloured glass. We can play a game with marbles.

lily
A lily is a plant with a large beautiful flower.

line

A line is a long mark that we draw with a pen or pencil. This pencil has drawn a line.

lion
A lion is a strong wild cat. The male lion has a main of hair around his face.

log

A log is a heavy stick of wood. We cut logs from the branches or the trunk of a tree.

lollipop
A lollipop is a hard sweet on a stick. We lick lollipops.

lunch

Lunch is a meal that we eat in the middle of the day.

m

M

m

match
A match is a small stick with a tip that burns. When we scratch a match it will burn.

meat

Meat is the flesh of animals. We eat meat. It is a food.

milk
Milk is a white liquid food that we drink. We get milk from cows, goats or sheep.

M m

N n

milkman
A milkman is a person who brings milk to us every day.

mirror
A mirror is a glass in which we can see ourselves.

mitten
A mitten is a glove with one part for the fingers and a smaller part for the thumb.

monkey
A monkey is a small animal that lives in trees. Monkeys have long tails.

monument
A monument is something we build to remember an event or a person. A monument is often a statue.

moon
The moon goes round the earth. We see the moon shining at night. Sometimes we see all of it. At other times we see part of it.

nail
A nail is a piece of metal with a flat head and a sharp point. A nail fastens pieces of wood together.

napkin
We use a napkin to keep our clothes clean when we eat. It is made of cloth or paper.

neck
The neck is the bit of the body that joins the head to the shoulders.

mop
We use a mop to clean floors. A mop has ropes or cloth at the end of a long handle.

mountain
A mountain is a piece of rock that is very high.

mouse
A mouse is a small animal that is grey or brown. Mice like to eat cheese.

mouth
The mouth is an opening in the face through which we speak and eat.

mug
A mug is a tall cup with a handle. We drink liquids from a mug.

music
Music is sound that is pleasing to hear. When we sing we make music. We also make music with musical instruments.

needle
A needle has a sharp point at one end and a hole at the other for thread. We sew with a needle.

nest
A nest is where birds and some animals live. It is their home. This is a bird's nest with three eggs in it.
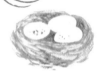

newspaper
A newspaper is what we read to find out what is happening. News is printed on paper in a newspaper.

number

We count things with numbers. A number tells us how many there are. There are six numbers here.

ocean

An ocean is a large area of salt water. The earth has five oceans.

office

An office is a place where we go to work.

onion

An onion is a vegetable that grows in the ground. It has a strong taste.

orange

An orange is a fruit that grows on trees in warm countries. The colour of an orange is also called orange.

pail

A pail is round and has a handle. We carry things like water or sand in a pail.

paintbox

A paintbox has paints in it. We use paints to colour things.

palm

A palm is a tree that grows in warm places. Coconuts grow on a coconut palm.

pan

A pan is what we use to cook food in. A pan is round and is made of metal. It has a handle so that we can lift it.

nut

A nut is a kind of fruit with a hard outside, or shell. We eat the inside, or kernel, of a nut. Nuts grow on trees.

ostrich

An ostrich is a large bird that cannot fly. It has beautiful feathers and lives in warm countries. It can run very fast.

overalls

We wear overalls over other clothes to keep them clean when we work or play.

overcoat

An overcoat is a long, coat that we wear outdoors in cold weather to keep us warm.

owl

An owl is a large bird with big, round eyes. Owls fly mostly at night. Some owls make a hooting noise.

pancake

A pancake is a thin flat cake made of flour, eggs and milk. It is cooked in a pan.

panther

A panther is a large, fierce wild cat. Some panthers are black in colour.

paper

Paper is what we write on. The pages of this book are paper. We can also make things with paper.

parachute

A parachute looks like an umbrella. When we jump from a plane, the parachute floats in the air and carries us down to the earth.

parade
When we parade, we are marching. When people march together they form a parade.

parrot

A parrot is a bird with bright feathers and a large bill. A parrot can say words.

paste
We use paste to join things together. We paste them together.

peach

A peach is a round fruit with a soft fuzzy yellow skin. Peaches are full of juice and are delicious to eat.

peanut
A peanut is a nut that grows in a shell under the ground. Peanuts are good to eat.

pear

A pear is a fruit that is round at one end. Some pears are green and some are brown in colour.

peas
A pea is a small round green vegetable. Peas grow in a long green pod.

pen
We write or draw with a pen. Ink in the pen comes out through a point at one end.

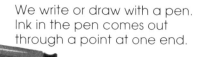

pencil
A pencil is a stick with lead in the middle. We write and draw with a pencil.

petal
A petal is the coloured part of a flower that looks like a leaf.

piano

A piano is made of wood and has black and white keys that make music when we press them.

picnic
A picnic is a meal that we eat out of doors in the sunshine. We have fun when we picnic.

picture

We make a picture by painting or drawing something or by taking a photograph of it. This book is full of pictures.

pie
A pie is food. When we bake fruit or meat in or under pastry made from flour and butter, we call it a pie.

pig

A pig is a fat animal that lives on a farm. Pork and bacon are meat from pigs.

pigeon

A pigeon is a bird. Many pigeons live in cities. We can train some pigeons to carry messages.

pineapple
A pineapple is a large fruit that grows on the ground in warm places. It has a thick skin.

pipe

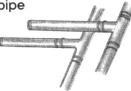

Water comes into our houses through a pipe. A pipe is a long tube.

piston
A piston is a round piece of metal that slides up and down in a pipe and makes things move in an engine.

plate

A plate is a flat dish. We eat food from a plate.

plug
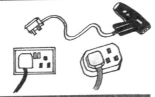
A plug fits into a hole. A machine has a plug to make it work.

plum

A plum is a fruit with a smooth skin. Plums are red, green or yellow. Plums are good to eat.

polar bear

A polar bear is a large wild animal that lives near the North Pole.

policeman

A policeman is a person who protects us from people who break the law.

queen

A queen is a woman who rules a country. The wife of a king is also called a queen.

rabbit

A rabbit is an animal with long pointed ears and strong back legs to help it jump.

race

These boys are running a race. The boy who runs fastest will win the race.

pony

A pony is a small horse. It is fun to ride on a pony. Children like ponies.

popcorn

Popcorn is a kind of corn that bursts open with a pop when we heat it.

potato

A potato is a vegetable that grows under ground. Chips and crisps are made from potatoes.

pulley

A pulley is a wheel with a groove in its edge for a rope. We use pulleys to lift heavy things.

puppy

A puppy is a very young dog. Puppies are fun to play with.

purr

When a kitten is happy it purrs. A purr is a sound like a hum.

quilt

A quilt is a cover for a bed. A quilt has something soft inside to keep us warm.

radio

Radio is a way of sending sounds by using radio waves in the air. A radio gives us news and music.

radish

A radish is a vegetable whose root is good to eat. We eat radishes in a salad.

R

rain
Rain is water that falls from the clouds in tiny drops. Rain makes us wet.

rainbow

When the sun shines through rain, it makes a rainbow. There are many colours in a rainbow.

raincoat
We wear a raincoat to keep us dry. A raincoat is made of cloth that keeps out the rain.

rake

We use a rake to gather up leaves. It has a long handle and an end that looks like a comb.

raspberry
A raspberry is a red berry – a small fruit that grows on a bush. We make delicious jam from raspberries.

rat

A rat is like a large black or brown mouse. Rats have strong teeth.

rattle
A rattle is a toy for a baby. When you shake a rattle, it makes a noise.

referee

A referee is a person who makes sure that a game is played properly. He makes us follow the rules.

refrigerator
A refrigerator is a kind of cupboard for keeping food cold. It is also called a fridge.

reindeer
A reindeer is a wild animal with large horns. Reindeer live in cold countries.

rhinoceros

A rhinoceros is a large wild animal with a thick skin. Rhinoceroses have one or two tusks on their noses.

ribbon
A ribbon is a long, narrow band of cloth or paper. Some girls wear a ribbon in their hair.

ring

A ring is a piece of jewellery that we wear on our fingers.

river
A river is what we call the water that flows towards the sea or ocean. A small river is called a stream.

road

A road is what we travel along to go from one place to another.

robin
A robin is a small bird with red feathers on its front. Robins sing a cheerful song.

rock

Rock is a hard stone or a large stone. Mountains are made of rock. We throw rocks.

roof
A roof is what covers the top of a building and keeps out the rain. All houses have roofs.

R

roller skate
A roller skate is a piece of metal with wheels that we put over our shoes. When we wear them we roll along.

rose

A rose is a flower that grows on a bush. Roses are red, yellow, pink or white. Some roses have a lovely smell.

rolling pin

A rolling pin is a round piece of wood. We use a rolling pin to make dough flat before we bake it.

rudder

A rudder is a flat piece of metal at the back of a plane or ship that it steers.

rooster

A rooster is a large male chicken with a loud call. A rooster is also called a cockerel.

ruler

A ruler is a flat stick with numbers on it for measuring. We also use a ruler to draw a line.

rope

A rope is a strong thick cord. We use a rope for skipping. A skipping rope has handles.

rug

We put a rug on the floor to keep our feet warm. Rugs are made of cloth.

S

sack

A sack is a large bag that we use to carry things in. There are oats in this sack.

sand

We can see sand at the seaside. It is made of tiny bits of stone. It is fun to play in the sand.

sail

A sail is what we call the canvas cloth on the mast of a yacht. Sails catch the wind and move the yacht along. They make the yacht sail.

sandwich

When we put cheese or meat between two pieces of bread we make a sandwich. We eat sandwiches on a picnic.

sailor

A sailor is a person who works on a ship or who sails in a yacht.

Santa Claus

Santa Claus is a person who lives at the North Pole. He brings us gifts at Christmas.

salad

A salad is a mixture of cold foods. A salad has raw vegetables, fruits, and cooked meat in it.

saw

A saw is a tool that we use to cut wood. It has a metal blade with sharp teeth.

salt

Salt is a white grainy substance that we use to flavour food. We keep salt in a salt cellar. Salt is found in the sea.

scales

When we want to find out how heavy a thing is, we put it on scales. Scales measure its weight.

scarecrow

A scarecrow is a figure that farmers put in fields to scare away the birds that eat the corn.

school

A school where we go to learn.

scissors

Scissors have two sharp blades. We use scissors to cut things like paper and cloth.

screw

A screw is a kind of nail. Screws have ridges so that they turn when they are put into wood.

seal

A seal is an animal that lives in the sea and on land. Seals have flippers to help them swim.

seesaw

A seesaw is a long board whose ends go up and down. We play on a seesaw.

sheep

A sheep is an animal that lives on a farm. We get meat and wool from sheep.

shelf

A shelf is a flat piece of wood on which we keep things. We keep books on bookshelves.

shell

A shell is the hard part on the outside of nuts, eggs and some animals. This is the shell of a sea animal. It is a sea shell.

ship

A ship is a large boat that sails on the sea.

shirt

A shirt is what we wear as clothes on the upper part of our bodies. Shirts are made of cloth.

shoe

A shoe is a covering for the foot. Shoes are usually made of leather.

shop

A shop is a place where we can buy things. Shops are run by shopkeepers.

shovel

A shovel is what we use to lift and move things like coal or snow. We shovel things.

sign

A sign tells us which way to go. We read what it says on a sign. This sign is pointing to the zoo.

skirt

A skirt is the part of a dress that hangs from the waist. Skirts are what girls wear as clothes.

sky

The sky is the air high above us. We see the sun, the moon, clouds and stars in the sky.

sledge

A sledge is a board that slides over snow. It has flat blades that are called runners.

S

slide

When we slide, we move smoothly and easily. Children like to slide down a slide.

slipper
A slipper is a soft shoe that we wear indoors. Here are two slippers for our feet.

snail

A snail is a small animal that has a shell. Snails live in the sea or in the garden, where they move very slowly.

snake
A snake is a long animal that has no legs. Snakes move by crawling along the ground.

snow

Snow is frozen rain. Snow falls from the sky as white flakes.

snowman
A snowman is a figure that we make from snow that lies on the ground.

soap

Soap is what we use to wash things. We wash clothes in soap powder and we wash ourselves with a bar of soap.

sock

A sock is a covering for the foot. We wear socks under our shoes.

sofa
A sofa is a chair that two people can sit on side by side. It has a back and arms at each end.

soldier
A soldier is a person who is in the army. Soldiers protect us from our enemies.

spade
A spade is a kind of shovel. It has a blade and a handle. We use spades to dig earth.

spider
A spider is a tiny animal that has eight legs. Spiders spin webs to catch insects for food.

spoon
A spoon is a little bowl with a long handle. We eat liquid food like soup with a spoon.

spring
A spring is a long piece of metal that is twisted into circles. Springs are pushed down by heavy weights.

squirrel
A squirrel is a small animal with a bushy tail. Squirrels live in trees and eat nuts. Squirrels are red or grey.

stairway

A stairway is a set of steps that we walk up to go from one level to another.

stamp
A stamp is what we put on a letter so the post office will send it where we want it to go.

star

At night we can see stars twinkling in the sky. A star is like the sun but is much farther away from us.

station
A station is a place where trains stop so that people can get on or get off.

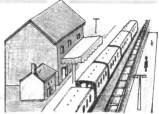

statue
A statue is a figure made of stone, wood or metal. This is a famous stone statue in Egypt, called the Sphinx.

stencil

A stencil has holes in it. When you spread paint across a stencil, a picture shows underneath.

stepladder
A stepladder is a ladder with flat steps instead of rungs. It has an extra support at the back so that it can stand.

stick
A stick is a long thin piece of wood. Things that look like sticks are also called sticks.

stirrup
A stirrup is part of the saddle of a horse. The stirrups are where we put our feet.

stone

Stone is the hard rock that we find in the ground. A stone is also a piece of this that we pick up and throw.

stool

A stool is a chair without a back or arms. We sit on a stool.

stopwatch
A stopwatch is a watch with a button that stops the hands. We use it to measure the time that something takes.

stork
A stork is a large bird with long legs and a long neck. Storks like to wade in water.

Straw is the dry stems of wheat. Farmers use straw to make beds for their cows.

street
A street is a road in a town or city. There are buildings along the sides of streets.

string

String is a thin rope that we use to tie up things. We tie up parcels with string.

sugar
Sugar is what we put in food to make it sweet. We keep sugar in a bowl.

suit
A suit is what men and women wear as clothes. A suit has a short coat and trousers or a skirt.

sun
The sun is the brightest thing in the sky. It gives us light and heat. The earth goes round the sun.

sweater
A sweater is what we wear as clothes to keep us warm. Sweaters are made of wool.

swing
A swing is a seat that hangs so that it moves back and forward. Children like to swing on a swing.

table
A table has a flat top and four legs. We put things on a table. We eat at a table.

tag

A tag is a small piece of paper or card that we tie on a parcel to tell who the parcel is for.

tail
A tail is a long part that grows at the back of many animals. This squirrel has a bushy tail.

tambourine
A tambourine is a small drum. We make music with a tambourine by tapping and shaking it.

taxi

A taxi is a car for hire. We pay the driver of a taxi to take us where we want to go.

teapot

Tea is a drink made with hot water and the leaves of a plant. We make tea in a teapot.

teddy bear
A teddy bear is a toy that looks like a bear. Teddy bears are furry and fun to cuddle.

telephone

A telephone carries your voice to another telephone far away.

television
Television is a way of sending pictures by using radio waves or cable. Television is also called TV.

tent
A tent is a large piece of heavy cloth that we sleep under when we sleep out of doors.

thimble

When you sew with a needle, you wear a thimble so that you don't prick your finger.

thistle
A thistle is a plant with a purple flower. Thistles have prickles so they are hard to pick.

thread

Thread is what we use with a needle when we sew. Thread is a very thin cord.

tiger
A tiger is a fierce wild cat. Tigers are yellow with black stripes.

time

What is the time? It is ten minutes past ten. Seconds, minutes and hours are the way we measure time.

toad
A toad is like a frog. Toads live on land but they also like to be in water.

toe
A toe is one of the parts at the end of our feet. We have five toes on each foot.

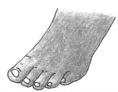

tomato
A tomato is the fruit of a tomato plant. Tomatoes are red and are good to eat in salads.

toothbrush

A toothbrush is a small brush with a long handle that we use to clean our teeth.

tool

A tool is what we use to help us work. We use garden tools when we work in the garden.

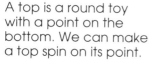

top

A top is a round toy with a point on the bottom. We can make a top spin on its point.

toy

A toy is what children play with. These are toys — a drum, a ball, a truck, two blocks, and a pail.

track

A track is what a train moves on. A track is made of two long metal rails on the ground.

tractor

A tractor is a machine that farmers use. It has big wheels so that it can move over rough ground.

train

A train is a line of coaches pulled by an engine. Trains carry us from one station to another.

tree

A tree is a large plant with green leaves and a thick stem that we call a trunk. Tree trunks give us wood.

umbrella

We use an umbrella to keep off the rain. Umbrellas fold up when we do not need to use them.

tricycle

A tricycle is a bicycle with three wheels. We ride a tricycle before we ride a bicycle.

truck

A truck is a large vehicle that carries things from place to place.

trunk

A trunk is a large box with a lid that we put things in. A trunk is also a part of an elephant and the stem of a tree.

tug

A tug is a small boat with a large engine. Tugs help to move big ships in harbour.

turkey

A turkey is a large bird. We eat turkey on Christmas Day.

turnip

A turnip is a plant with a large root that grows under the ground. The root is a vegetable that we eat.

turtle

A turtle is an animal with a shell. Turtles live in water.

typewriter

A typewriter is a machine for writing. When you press a key, it prints a letter.

underwear

Underwear is what we wear under clothes and next to the skin.

vacuum cleaner
A vacuum cleaner is a machine that we use to clean carpets. It sucks the dirt out of carpets.

vegetable
A vegetable is a plant with parts that we eat. We eat the leaves, the seeds or the roots of vegetables.

valentine

A valentine is a card we send to someone we like very much on St. Valentine's Day, 14th February.

violet

A violet is a tiny plant with a very pretty flower .

vase

A vase is a kind of jar. We put flowers into water in a vase.

violin

We make music with a violin by pulling a bow across its strings. It is a musical instrument.

waiter

A waiter is a person who brings us a meal in a restaurant.

weasel

A weasel is a small animal that has short legs and soft brown fur. Weasels eat birds, mice and rabbits.

walrus

A walrus is a large animal that lives in the sea. Walruses have two long, pointed tusks.

whale

A whale is a large animal that lives in the sea. Whales breathe through a hole in their heads.

wall

A wall is the side of a house or a room. Most houses and rooms have four walls.

wheat

Wheat is a plant that grows a grain that is made into flour. We make bread from flour.

wash

When we wash things, we make them clean. We wash things with soap and water.

wheel

A wheel is round and turns. A bicycle needs two wheels to move. A car needs four wheels.

watch
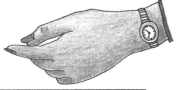
A watch is a small clock that we wear on the wrist. Watches tell us the time.

wheelbarrow

We use a wheelbarrow to move things. It has one wheel, two legs, and two handles.

watermelon

A watermelon is a very large fruit. Watermelons are green on the outside and pink inside.

whistle

When we blow into a whistle, it makes a sound. Whistles are made of metal or wood.

wig

A wig is like a hat. A wig is a covering of false hair for the head.

windmill

A windmill has sails that catch the wind and move machinery to pump water or grind corn.

window

A window is an opening in a wall with glass in it. Light comes through a window.

witch

A witch is an imaginary person, like an elf. Witches fly through the air on brooms and wear tall, pointed hats.

X-ray

An X-ray is a kind of light that goes through our bodies to make sure we are well.

yacht

A yacht is a boat with sails. Some yachts have engines and are called motor yachts.

yawn

When you open your mouth and take a long breath, you are yawning. People yawn when they are tired.

zebra

A zebra is a wild animal that looks like a horse. Zebras have black and white stripes on their bodies.

zigzag

A zigzag is a shape with short, sharp turns. This sweater has a zigzag pattern on it.

wolf

A wolf is a large wild animal that looks like a big dog. Wolves hunt in groups.

woman

A woman is a grown-up female person. Mummy is a woman. A girl grows up to be a woman.

world

The world is the earth and everything that is on it. The world is round.

wreath

A wreath is a ring of leaves or flowers that we hang on the door at Christmas to welcome people.

xylophone

We make music on a xylophone by hitting its metal keys with a little hammer.

yellow

Yellow is a colour. Here a paint brush is painting the colour yellow.

youth

Youth is when we are young. Tommy is a youth. He is older than a boy and not yet a man.

zip

A zip is a way of fastening clothes. A zip is long and has two lines of teeth that join.

zoo

A zoo is a place where we keep wild animals in cages so that people can see them.